JAN   2009

I Love to Draw Dogs!

Jennifer Lipsey

LARK BOOKS
A Division of Sterling Publishing Co., Inc.
New York / London

My Very Favorite Art Book

For Oliver, my sweet little animal lover, and Frankie, his sweet little doggie.

Editors
JOE RHATIGAN &
VERONIKA GUNTER

Creative Director
CELIA NARANJO

Lipsey, Jennifer.
  My very favorite art book : I love to draw dogs! / Jennifer Lipsey. -- 1st ed.
      p. cm.
  Includes index.
  ISBN 978-1-60059-153-2 (hc-plc with jacket : alk. paper)
  1. Dogs in art--Juvenile literature. 2. Drawing--Technique--Juvenile literature. I. Title. II. Title: I love to draw dogs!
    NC783.8.D64L57 2008
    704.9'4329772--dc22

                2008016439

10 9 8 7 6 5 4 3 2 1

First Edition

Published by Lark Books, A Division of
Sterling Publishing Co., Inc.
387 Park Avenue South, New York, NY 10016

© 2008, Jennifer Lipsey

Distributed in Canada by Sterling Publishing,
c/o Canadian Manda Group, 165 Dufferin Street
Toronto, Ontario, Canada M6K 3H6

Distributed in the United Kingdom by GMC Distribution Services,
Castle Place, 166 High Street, Lewes, East Sussex, England BN7 1XU
Distributed in Australia by Capricorn Link (Australia) Pty Ltd.,
P.O. Box 704, Windsor, NSW 2756 Australia

If you have questions or comments about this book, please contact:

Lark Books
67 Broadway
Asheville, NC 28801
828-253-0467

Manufactured in China

ISBN 13: 978-1-60059-153-2

For information about custom editions, special sales, and premium and corporate purchases, please contact Sterling Special Sales Department at 800-805-54 89 or specialsales@sterlingpub.com.

Contents

It's Fun to Draw Dogs! • 4

Border Collie • 6

Labrador Retriever • 8

Parson Russell Terrier • 10

French Bulldog • 11

Golden Retriever • 12

Maltese • 13

Dachshund • 14

West Highland White Terrier • 16

Basset Hound • 17

Siberian Husky • 18

Dalmatian • 20

Pomeranian • 22

Boxer • 23

Pug • 24

Scottish Terrier • 25

Shih Tzu • 26

Beagle • 27

Yorkshire Terrier • 28

Chihuahua • 30

Great Dane • 31

German Shepherd • 32

Shetland Sheepdog • 34

Cocker Spaniel • 35

Doberman Pinscher • 36

Miniature Schnauzer • 37

Bulldog • 38

Old English Sheepdog • 39

Poodle • 40

Wolf • 42

Mixed Breeds • 44

Dogs in Action • 46

Index • 48

It's Fun to Draw Dogs!

People love dogs and dogs love people. They have been friends for thousands of years.

Have you always wanted to draw dogs that look real? This book will show you more than 40 different ways to draw your furry friends.

Don't worry if your drawings don't look just like the dogs in the book.

Just practice and have FUN!

You will get lots of
ideas for different
dogs and poses.

Big dogs...

...jumping dogs...

...little dogs...

...and even
skating dogs!

Here's how to draw the pictures in this book:

1.

2.

3.

4.

Use a pencil to follow
all the pink steps to
draw a dog.

Go over the lines you
want to keep in black
marker or pen.

Erase the extra
pencil lines.

Color it!
This book uses markers.
Crayons or colored pencils
work well too!

Now let's draw Dogs!

Border Collie

This dog has an instinct to manage and guide other animals.
It's very smart and has lots of energy.

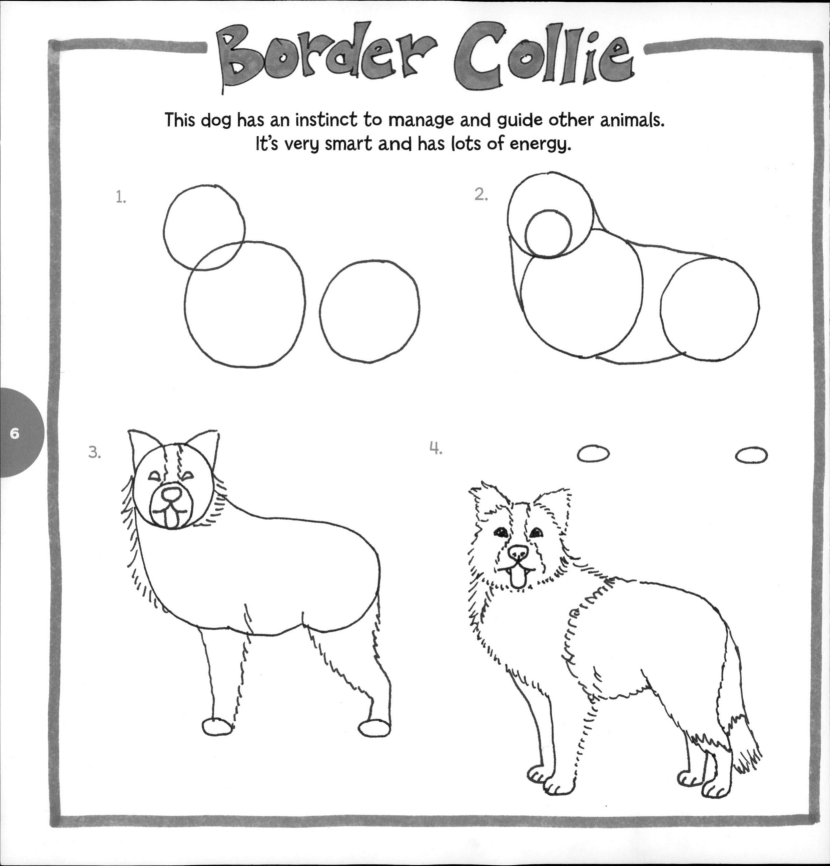

1.

2.

3.

4.

The Border Collie is an excellent sheepherder.

To get the sheep to move, the dog stares at them— instead of barking or biting. This is called giving eye.

Border Collies need lots of exercise. They love to have a job to do!

Labrador Retriever

This dog is smart, strong, and loving. It's one of the most popular breeds in the world.

Sitting

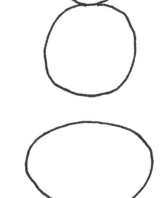

1.

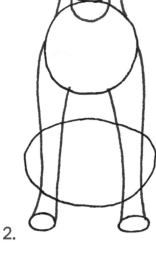

2.

3.

4.

Standing

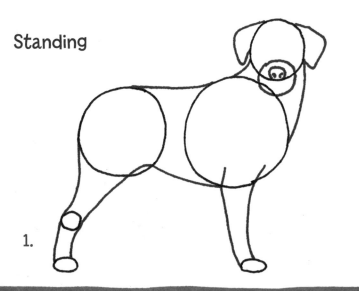

1.

2

The Labrador Retriever is a hard worker and is very good at any job a dog can do.

Labs love to swim, retrieve, and run!

Labs can be solid black, chocolate, or yellow.

Parson Russell Terrier

Parson Russell Terriers are lively little dogs who love to play with toys.

Lying down

1.

2.

3.

4.

Standing

1.

2.

This breed is also known as the Jack Russell Terrier.

3.

French Bulldog

The French Bulldog has a short body and big, bat-like ears.

1.

2.

3.

4.

Frenchies love to play and cuddle.
They also make great house pets.

Golden Retriever

This dog is named for its soft, gleaming coat—and its fondness for fetching!

1.

2.

3.

This gentle, smart breed is used as a rescue dog and guide dog.

4.

Goldens love kids and other animals—and swimming!

Maltese

The Maltese is a very small, playful dog. It has big, dark eyes,
a black nose, and beautiful white hair.

1.

2.

3.

4.

The Maltese is an
old breed. It's been
around more than
3,500 years!

Dachshund

Dachshunds are long, short dogs. They were once used as hunting dogs to get into deep burrows.

Sitting, Front View

1.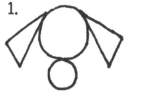
2.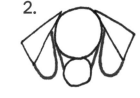
3.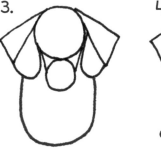
4.
5.

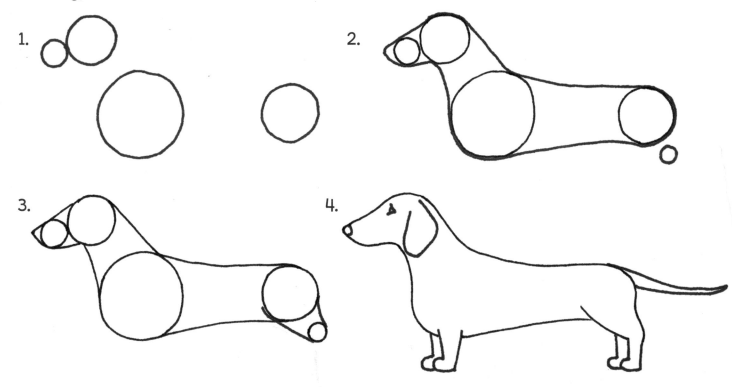

Standing, Side View

1.

2.

3.

4.

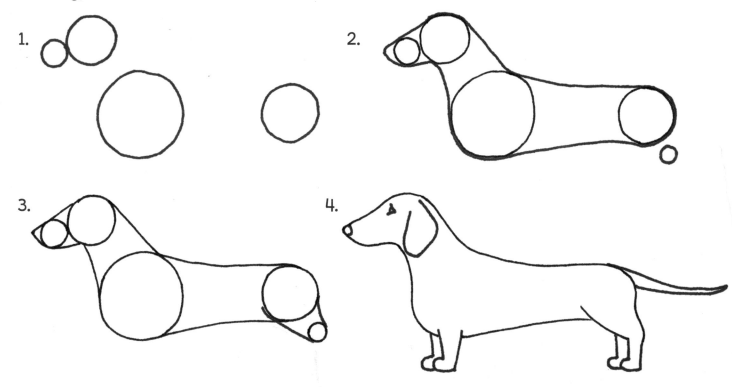

Try a sitting Dachshund with a side view of the head.

How about a long-haired Dachshund?

Dachshunds have nicknames like sausage dog, wiener dog, and hot dog. Why do you think that is?

The most common colors are red or black with tan markings.

West Highland White Terrier

Often called Westies, these small dogs have wiry hair and love to explore.

1.

2.

This little dog is frisky, friendly, and loves to play.

3.

4.

Basset Hound

The friendly Basset Hound has a droopy face, long ears, and very short legs.

1.

2.

3.

4.

Basset Hounds have a remarkable sense of smell. And they can drool a lot!

Siberian Husky

The Siberian Husky is a strong and beautiful dog. It can haul heavy loads over great distances in very cold weather.

1.

2.

3.

Siberians are known for their wolf-like features.

4.

Siberians love to work. Try drawing a team of sled dogs.

This breed carries its tail up when it's active.

The Siberian Husky can have blue eyes, brown eyes, or both!

Their puppies are cute! They look like bear cubs!

Dalmatian

These spotted dogs need LOTS of exercise every day.

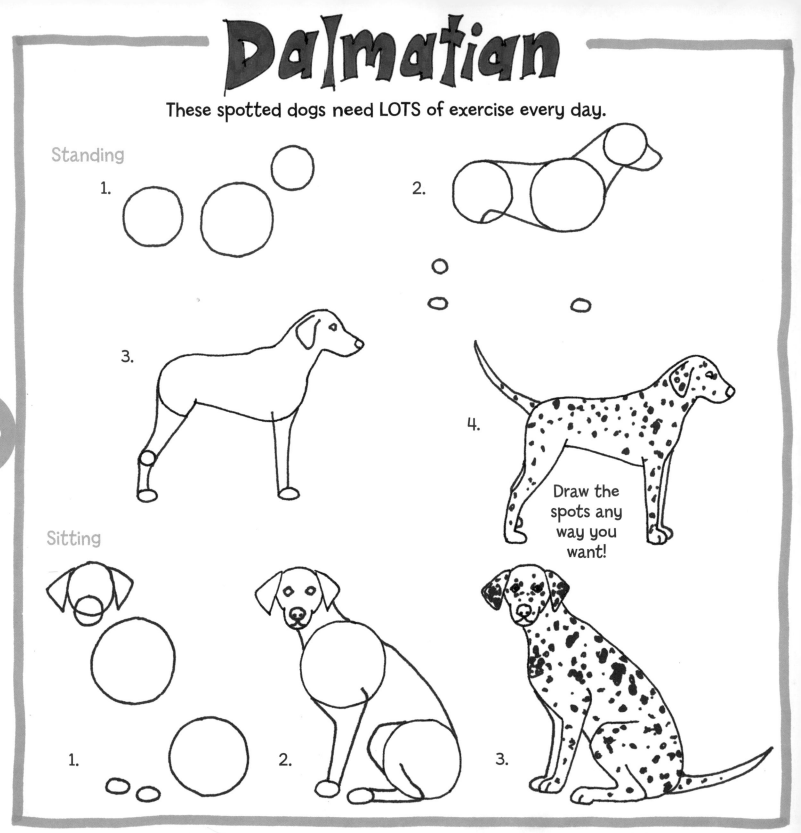

Standing

1.

2.

3.

4. Draw the spots any way you want!

Sitting

1.

2.

3.

Dalmatians are best known as firehouse mascots.

Dalmatian puppies are born white. Their spots develop later and can be any of eight different colors!

Dalmatians have done many jobs and have even starred in movies.

Pomeranian

This tiny, fluffy dog is curious and happy.

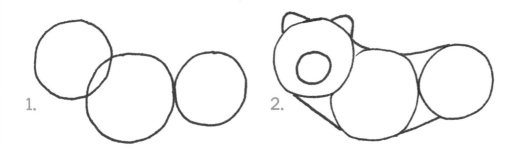

1.

2.

The Pomeranian has a fox-like face, but its ancestors are big, furry sled dogs.

3.

4.

The Pomeranian's loud bark makes it a good watchdog.

Boxer

The Boxer is a medium-sized, short-haired dog. It's very loyal, likes to play, and has lots of love to give.

1.

2.

3.

4.

Boxers make great family dogs, as well as police and military dogs.

Pug

Pugs are happy, playful dogs with wrinkled, squished-looking faces.

Front

1.

2.

3.

4.

Side

1.

2.

Pugs snore
and can snort
like a pig.

3.

24

Scottish Terrier

These short-legged dogs have wiry coats. They're nicknamed Scotties.

1.

2.

3.

4.

This dog is brave and stubborn, and it loves its human family above all else!

Shih Tzu

Shih Tzu (say it "shee tsoo") means lion in Chinese.

1.

2.

This breed has long, beautiful hair that some people trim to make grooming easier.

3.

4.

Shih Tzu puppies are so cute!

Beagle

Beagles are small hound dogs that like to bark, howl, and bay.

1.

2.

3.

This affectionate breed is one of the most popular family pets.

4.

A beagle named Uno is famous for winning the Westminster Dog Show in 2008.

Yorkshire Terrier

The Yorkshire Terrier, or Yorkie, is a very small dog with long hair.
Yorkies are the most popular small dogs in many countries.

Front

1. 2. 3. 4. 5.

Side

1. 2. 3.

Puppy

1. 2. 3. 4. 5.

Try drawing some cute Yorkie puppies.

A Yorkie can have a short haircut.

Yorkies have long silky coats that are bluish black on the back and tail. The head, chest, and feet are gold.

29

Yorkies like to go everywhere with their owners.

Chihuahua

The tiny Chihuahua is the world's smallest dog!

1.

2.

The smallest Chihuahuas are no larger than a soda can!

This dog can be any color and can have short or long hair.

3.

4.

Great Dane

This gentle giant is the world's tallest dog.

1.

2.

3.

4.

The Great Dane is friendly and loving.

A Great Dane's coat can be brown, blue, black, or harlequin (white with black patches).

German Shepherd

This popular dog is smart, strong, and loyal.

Standing

1.

2.

3.

4.

Lying Down

1.

2.

3.

Here are some jobs
German Shepherds do well:
Search & rescue dog
Seeing-eye dog
Guard dog
Police dog
Military dog

With careful training,
this dog can make a
wonderful pet.

Shetland Sheepdog

This small dog (nicknamed Sheltie) is very playful and intelligent.

1.

2.

3.

4.

The Sheltie has a long, fluffy coat.

This dog is a great sheepdog and family pet.

Cocker Spaniel

The Cocker Spaniel is a happy dog with silky hair and long, floppy ears.

1.

2.

3.

4.

This breed is a favorite show dog.

Doberman Pinscher

The Doberman Pinscher is a powerful and quick dog.

1.

2.

3.

4.

Most Dobermans are black and brown.

Miniature Schnauzer

A bushy beard and eyebrows give these small dogs their special look.

1.

2.

3.

4.

Miniature Schnauzers can be black, black with silver, and salt and pepper.

These little guys are quick and like to have fun.

Bulldog

Bulldogs may look a little mean, but they are actually one of the gentlest dog breeds.

1.

2.

These guys have a short, heavy body and a broad chest.

3.

4.

Well-trained Bulldogs are calm around kids and pets.

Old English Sheepdog

This big, shaggy dog is hairy and fun to play with.

1.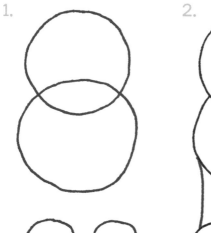

2.

3.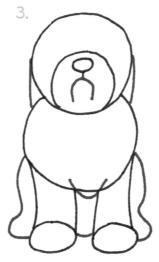

4.

Old English Sheepdogs sometimes herd people as if they were a flock of sheep.

Poodle

The poodle is considered one of the smartest of the dog breeds.

1.

2.

Standing

Poodles come in three sizes:

Small = Toy (under 7 pounds)

Medium = Miniature
(7 to 13 pounds)

Large = Standard
(45 to 70 pounds)

3.

4.

Poodles learn
tricks fast!

Sitting

1.

2.

3.

Draw small bumps
to make the hair
look curly.

Many dogs enjoy backpacking—just like humans! The Standard Poodle especially loves children.

Poodles often win awards at dog shows and in dog sports. This Poodle has a special haircut called a show clip.

Poodles have hair—not fur. This means they don't shed. They can be any solid color such as black, brown, white, or gray.

Wolf

The beautiful and mysterious ancestor of the dog has existed since the Ice Age.

1.

2.

3.

4.

A wolf can weigh from 40 to 175 pounds.

Wolves have appeared in art and stories for thousands of years.

Wolves communicate by howling.

The whole pack helps raise the pups.

Mixed Breeds

These are dogs whose parents are not from the same breed.
Some of the best pets around are mixed breeds—affectionately known as "mutts."

Sometimes two breeds are mixed to create a hybrid or crossbreed dog.

Like this:

 **+**  **=**

Labrador Retriever (page 8)

Poodle (page 40)

Labradoodle

Here are some other hybrids:
Golden Doodle (Golden Retriever & Poodle)
Cockapoo (Cocker Spaniel & Poodle)
Maltipoo (Maltese & Poodle)
Puggle (Pug & Beagle)

Poodles are popular for making hybrids because they don't shed.

If you want a pet dog, consider adopting one from an animal shelter, where there are lots of awesome dogs—like this little guy, Ira!—waiting for a family to love.

Can you guess what kinds of dogs are in Ira's family tree? Who knows! But he sure is cute.

Have fun drawing your own mixed breeds and mutts.
Use the different dogs in this book for help.

This little guy has a Pug body and tail (page 24), a Chihuahua head (page 30), and Parson Russell Terrier markings (page 10).

This furry girl just wants to have fun.

This funny mix has a Basset Hound body (page 17), Cocker Spaniel ears (page 35), and Dalmatian spots (page 20).

This big boy has a Boxer face (page 23), Retriever ears (page 12), and German Shepherd body and coat (page 32).

Dogs in Action

Dogs love to play, work, exercise, and keep us company!

Dogs like to have fun—just like you!

Try drawing a dog doing something.
Use the body circles to help.

Some dogs
love to dig!

Some dogs are good
at doing tricks.

Therapy dogs help sick or
hurt people feel better.

Dogs have lots of jobs:

Guide Dogs
Sled Dogs
Guard Dogs
Therapy Dogs
Mascots
Search & Rescue Dogs

Police Dogs
Herding Dogs
Hunting Dogs
Stunt Dogs
Movie Stars

Dogs can be
awesome athletes.

Many dogs like to play
catch. Have you ever
seen a Frisbee dog?

Dog Agility is a popular dog
sport. Humans tell their dogs
how to go through an obstacle
course. The fastest dog wins.

Did you know that some dogs
can surf, skimboard and ride
skateboards?! Dogs rock!

Index

Basset Hound, 17
Beagle, 27
Border Collie, 6-7
Boxer, 23
Bulldog, 38

Chihuahua, 30
Cocker Spaniel, 35

Dachshund, 14-15
Dalmatian, 20-21
Doberman Pinscher, 36
Dog Agility, 47
Dog Jobs, 46
Dogs in Action, 46-47

French Bulldog, 11
Frenchies. See French Bulldog

German Shepherd, 32-33
Golden Retriever, 12
Great Dane, 31

Jack Russell Terrier. See Parson
    Russell Terrier

Labradoodle, 44
Labrador Retriever, 8-9

Maltese, 13
Miniature Schnauzer, 37
Mixed Breeds, 44-45
Mutt, 44

Old English Sheepdog, 39

Parson Russell Terrier, 10
Pomeranian, 22
Poodle, 40-41
Pug, 24

Scotties. See Scottish Terrier
Scottish Terrier, 25
Sheltie. See Shetland Sheepdog
Shetland Sheepdog, 34
Shih Tzu, 26
Siberian Husky, 18-19

Therapy Dogs, 46

West Highland White Terrier, 16
Westies. See West Highland White
    Terrier
Wolf, 42-43

Yorkies. See Yorkshire Terrier
Yorkshire Terrier, 28-29